Published 2024
Printed in the United States of America

Paperback print ISBN: 979-8-218-45696-2

SCAN ME

Scan this QR code to claim your offer.

INTRODUCTION

Divorced and drowning in the online dating pool?

Lacking confidence with women?

Sick of wasting time and hard-earned cash on bad dates, catfish, and crazies?

Whether you've been dating like it's a second job, or you're newly single and unsure about diving back in, this workbook can *Change Your Luck With Women Forever.*

WHY DO THE WORK?

Through this self-actualizing journey, you will:

- Rebuild self-esteem and boost confidence with women.
- Get more women interested with less effort.
- Be desired for who you are.
- Find a woman who truly loves you.
- Achieve a deeply satisfying relationship.
- Save time and money by avoiding bad dates.
- Never be stuck in an unsatisfying relationship again.

THE CORE JOURNEY

This program helps newly divorced and chronically single men gain clarity and confidence to find the love they deserve. Here's what you'll delve into:

Part 1: Look Within

Your journey starts by looking within. Answer questions that shape how you perceive yourself and how you show up in relationships. This introspection lays the foundation for understanding the deeper aspects of your personality and relationship patterns.

Self-awareness is crucial. Understand your strengths and weaknesses, and identify the patterns that have hindered your relationships in the past. This section will help you confront your insecurities, recognize your worth, and build a stronger sense of self.

Part 2: Exorcising Your Exes

Next, you'll dive into past relationships to identify and overcome unhealthy patterns. Reflect on your past relationships, analyze what went wrong, and understand the dynamics that led to their failure.

This isn't about blaming your exes or yourself. It's about recognizing patterns and learning from them. By understanding these patterns, you can avoid repeating the same mistakes and build healthier relationships in the future.

Part 3: Your Ideal Woman & Ideal Relationship

Get clear on your ideals to save years and a ton of money chasing the wrong women! Define what you truly want in a partner and a relationship.

What qualities are non-negotiable for you? What values and interests do you want to share with your partner? This clarity will guide you in making better choices, cutting losses quickly, and attracting the right kind of women into your life.

Part 4: Evaluating Your Values

Harmony in relationships is easily achieved when the woman you're with shares your values. This section will show you how to leverage what you truly value to get the love you deserve.

Understand your core values and ensure they align with your partner's. When your values align, it creates a strong foundation for a lasting and fulfilling relationship.

Part 5: What Do You Want?

Gain confidence and clarity about your wants and needs. Uncertainty about what you want is one of the biggest dating pitfalls.

This section helps you define your needs and desires clearly. By knowing what you want, you can communicate effectively with potential partners and avoid wasting time on relationships that don't meet your needs.

Part 6: Conquering Your MalBes

Identify and conquer maladaptive beliefs (MalBes) that cause self-sabotage. Most of us have subconscious gremlins that hold us back.

These beliefs might stem from childhood, past relationships, or societal conditioning. This section will help you spot these beliefs, challenge them, and ultimately conquer them. By doing so, you'll stop self-sabotaging and start living authentically.

The 10 First Dates Challenge

Ready to date? Use the worksheets to track your thoughts on dates. Not ready? Work through the six sections first. You'll know when you're ready, and you'll see a huge difference.

Once I felt ready to date, I gave myself a challenge: to go on 10 first dates to knock the rust off and deploy my skillset. I put it into practice and was far more successful than I could have imagined.

The worksheets for your 10 First Dates Challenge refer to the work you did on yourself in the prior sections. If you are actively dating now, it's okay to keep going. Once you get through the first two sections of the workbook, begin using the 10 First Date Challenge Worksheets to track your thoughts on your dates.

But if you have been struggling with dating, or you're afraid to get out there, don't put any pressure on yourself to go on any new dates until you make it through the six main sections of the workbook. You will know when you're ready. You will see a HUGE difference in how you show up, how clear you are, and how the type of woman you want is so much easier to find.

BEFORE THIS WORKBOOK

This workbook began as a personal journey. It took me years of searching, reading, attending seminars, working with therapists, and listening to podcasts and audiobooks to figure out what was standing in my way of experiencing happy and fulfilling relationships.

I discovered that my lack of clarity was ultimately what was holding me back.
I applied my professional skills from my M&A (Mergers & Acquisitions) career to my personal life. By using a deliberate approach and blending it with management approaches like Geno Wickman's *Traction, Stephen Covey's 7 Habits*, and a Napoleon Hill-style mastermind, I boiled my five-year journey down to six core areas of inquiry.

This started as a series of worksheets I led multiple clients through. Every man who went through these workbooks reported it was revealing and paradigm-changing.

Dedicate yourself to get the workbook done in a week, or take your time to chip away at it over a couple of months. To keep you on track.

Scan the QR code to claim this offer.

THE SECRET INGREDIENT

Join a mastermind of men sharing common experiences. Our MAGO Gents Men's Groups help men transform into their ideal selves and gain clarity on who they are and what they need from relationships.

"The Men's Groups have been a total game-changer for me. Especially as I was going through my divorce. The support from the licensed facilitator and the other guys who've gone through the same thing has been amazing. I'm not ready to date again. But there's really no pressure. I'm just taking my time and doing work on me."

-CJ Fleming ★ ★ ★ ★ ★

We're a group of gentlemen devoted to helping other men heal emotionally, mentally, psychologically, and socially. We provide support as our members transform themselves into a more ideal version of themselves and get clarity on who they are and what they want and need.

YOUR CHOICE

Sit on the sidelines or transform your love life now. Attend your two free online groups, and if you have questions, email us at support@magogents.com. Dive in and start transforming your love life!

This program isn't about being an alpha male or a pickup artist. It's about doing deep work, living with integrity, and getting exactly what you want in your relationships. Dive in and Change Your Luck With Women Forever.

> "This program has been a true game changer for me at a fundamental level. Going beyond the dramatic improvements in the dating/relationship scene, the program has helped me attain a much deeper understanding of self that has also led to greater self-acceptance, self-esteem, and self-love. In turn, this has all permeated well beyond my dating/relationship life. It has been a veritable paradigm shift that has manifested in big changes in every important aspect of my life, including, of course, the ability to discern what truly matters. I highly recommend this program not only to anyone looking for a significant change in their dating life but also to anyone seeking a significant change in their relationship with themselves."
>
> ★ ★ ★ ★ ★
>
> - Serge B.

ADDITIONAL SUPPORT AND RESOURCES

To ensure that you get the maximum benefit from the workbooks, we've invited you to join us for two live group sessions led by a Most Amazing Group of Gentlemen Certified Facilitator. These small group sessions are powerful. You'll pick your regular night when you register. Scan the QR code. you need to claim your free sessions and schedule your onboarding call.

Start working on the workbooks and join two live in-person sessions in the next 30 days. There's no obligation. If at the end of those 30 days, you want to continue, you'll have an opportunity to. You have nothing to lose except your lack of clarity and confidence (which women can smell from a mile away).

So, if you're sick and tired of feeling overwhelmed and unsure, if you still haven't found what you're really looking for in your love life, dive into this DEEP WORK WORKBOOK.

Scan this QR code to claim your offer.

SCAN ME

COMMON CHALLENGES AND HOW TO OVERCOME THEM

During and after divorce or the end of any serious long-term relationship, a lot of men—especially those who have been beaten down emotionally by a difficult ex-wife—feel unlovable, broken, worthless, and hopeless. They lose their mojo and feel unsure of themselves, sometimes even scared of being vulnerable because of the pain and heartbreak they've endured.

Many men struggle to get out of the starting gate and get frustrated with dating once they dive in. They second-guess every move they make. If that sounds like you, you're going to want to dive into the workbooks right now.

Most men don't work on themselves. The guys who go through our programs and become full members of the Most Amazing Group of Gentlemen have an advantage over most guys out there. We're self-actualizing gentlemen who live in integrity and date by a code.

> **"It helped me to become the person I needed to be to attract the partner I desired."**
>
> **- Tim H.** ★★★★★

Beautiful, intelligent, high-value women—the type you might really want to date but probably think are out of your league—would go for you if you have the confidence and conviction of who you are. They're also not looking for people-pleasing, co-dependent simps. They're looking for good men who do the work on themselves.

Men who go through our program have a distinct advantage over most guys because we do the work. We know who we are. We know what we want. We know what we need. And we've learned to stand in our truth, live with integrity, and communicate our desires to finally get exactly what we want in our relationships with women.

Are you ready? Then dive in...
To Greater Love,

Mark Hirsch, Founder
MAGO Gents

Part 1
Look Within

WELCOME

Welcome to "Change Your Luck With Women Forever," a proven program of self-care and personal development that helps you transform how you show up in relationship with women. It might surprise you to find that this program isn't loaded with tips and techniques for picking up women or getting dates.

It's mostly about doing work on you. The work that you'll be doing will positively change how you show up in relationships, and the type of women you attract into your life... as well as how you relate to them.

We'll guide you and help you through the process.

Some of the questions are very personal. This work will make you feel uncomfortable. It will trigger you. At some point, you might be wondering why you're even doing this. This will take you out of your comfort zone. But rest assured, this process works. We guarantee it. So, let's forge ahead and learn more about you.

Answer honestly, and candidly. If there's anything you feel uncomfortable to put down in writing, just make a note to yourself and you can go over it in a private session with your MAGO Gents Coach or in an upcoming group. We are excited to have you beginning this process and look forward to seeing your transformation.

BASICS

Gentlemen

Name:

Email:

Mobile: | Age:

Height: | Weight:

What type of work do you do?

Relationship Status circle one (divorced, widowed, single) provide details such how long since you were divorced or widowed

Where are you from originally?

What is your educational background / what degrees and from where?

Change Your Luck With Women Forever

MORE ABOUT YOU

Summarize your parent's relationship with one another and what you observed about them growing up:

Describe your current relationship with each of your parents (if they are no longer living, describe what it was like prior to their passing):

Which one of your parents are / were you closest with?

Any siblings? If so, where do you fall in the birth order and describe your relationships with each sibling.

Change Your Luck With Women Forever

MORE ABOUT YOU

What are 3 qualities that you love about yourself?

What are 3 things you would change about yourself if you could?

Reach out to your closest friend (the person who knows you for the longest time) and ask them for 5 words that best describe you.

Which word did your friend use that surprised you most and why?

MORE ABOUT YOU

Detail one of your happiest memories as a child.

Detail one of the most embarrassing / humiliating things that has happened to you as an adult in regard to dating or in a relationship:

Detail the most traumatic experience of your childhood.

MORE ABOUT YOU

Rate yourself on a scale of physical attractiveness 1 - 10

Rate yourself in terms of "game" with women: 1 - 10

What is your biggest challenge when it comes to dating?

Describe in detail, what do you believe "all women" want in a relationship.

Complete the sentence: I could find happiness in a relationship IF I,

ASSESSMENT

Go to this link (https://www.16personalities.com/free-personality-test) and take the free test, then write below which of the 16 personality types you were classified as... it's a 4 letter type... with that, also explain how the type matches you, and at least one way the type does not match how you see yourself.

Which 4 letter type are you?

How does this type match you?

Describe at least one way that this type is a mismatch to how you see yourself and why.

You've made it to the end. Well done! This week's workbook required a lot of introspection. Some say these questions provoke interesting discoveries.

Share your personal discoveries and common experiences by participating in two free MAGO Gents groups, which are included with your purchase. To claim it, just click this link.

Change Your Luck With Women Forever

Gentlemen

Gentlemen

Change Your Luck With Women Forever

Part 2

Exorcising Your Exes

"EXORCISING" YOUR EXES

Explore your Exes Past.

Name the three most impactful romantic relationships in your life...

Name of most recent Ex:

Name of the prior Ex:

Name of third Ex:

INSTRUCTIONS FOR THE EXORCISE:

In three sessions, answer a series of 14 questions about each of your three Exes listed above.

You will be diving pretty deeply into your memory to fish for answers in some cases. So to keep it focused on one Ex at a time, it's important that you take, at least, a 20 minute break between each set of questions...

"EXORCISING" YOUR EXES

Start with Ex #1.

Sit back, and close your eyes and I want you to think about Ex #1 on your list, picture that person's face. Take a few seconds to sit with that image in your mind, then launch into the questions below.

1. What are three words that come up for you as you picture ex #1?

2. How long were you and ex #1 together?

Years   months

3. What was the best part of your relationship with ex #1?

4. What was the biggest challenge you faced during your relationship with ex #1?

5. What ultimately led to the end of your relationship with ex #1?

6. When you and ex #1 split up, what did that feel like for you?

"EXORCISING" YOUR EXES

7. What did you learn about yourself from your experience with ex #1?

8. What was the 1 thing you wish you knew about ex #1 before you got into that relationship?

9. How has your relationship with ex #1 affected your perspective on relationships today?

10. What did you and ex #1 disagree about the most during your relationship?

11. How did your friends and family feel about your relationship with ex #1?

12. What do you wish you had done differently during your relationship with ex #1?

13. Do you still have any contact with ex #1?

14. How do you feel about ex #1 now, and how has that changed over time?

Change Your Luck With Women Forever

"EXORCISING" YOUR EXES

Now, take a break for a little while at least 20 minutes. Do something that will clear Ex #1 out of your head.

When you come back, we will move onto ex #2.

Ex #2

Sit back, and close your eyes and I want you to think about the #2 on your list, picture that person's face.

1. What are three words that come up for you as you picture ex #2?

2. How long were you and ex #2 together?

[   ] Years [   ] months

3. What was the best part of your relationship with ex #2?

4. What was the biggest challenge you faced during your relationship with ex #2?

5. What ultimately led to the end of your relationship with ex #2?

6. When you and ex #2 split up, what did that feel like for you?

"EXORCISING" YOUR EXES

7. What did you learn about yourself from your experience with ex #2?

8. What was the 1 thing you wish you knew about ex #2 before you got into that relationship?

9. How has your relationship with ex #2 affected your perspective on relationships today?

10. What did you and ex #2 disagree about the most during your relationship?

11. How did your friends and family feel about your relationship with ex #2?

12. What do you wish you had done differently during your relationship with ex #2?

13. Do you still have any contact with ex #2?

14. How do you feel about ex #2 now, and how has that changed over time?

Change Your Luck With Women Forever

"EXORCISING" YOUR EXES

Now, take a break for a little while. And when you come back, we will move onto Ex #3.

Sit back, and close your eyes and I want you to think about the #3 on your list, picture that person's face.

1. What are three words that come up for you as you picture ex #3?

[ ] [ ] [ ]

2. How long were you and ex #3 together?

[ ] Years [ ] months

3. What was the best part of your relationship with ex #3?

[ ]

4. What was the biggest challenge you faced during your relationship with ex #3?

[ ]

5. What ultimately led to the end of your relationship with ex #3?

[ ]

6. When you and ex #3 split up, what did that feel like for you?

[ ]

7. What did you learn about yourself from your experience with ex #3?

8. What was the 1 thing you wish you knew about ex #3 before you got into that relationship?

9. How has your relationship with ex #3 affected your perspective on relationships today?

10. What did you and ex #3 disagree about the most during your relationship?

11. How did your friends and family feel about your relationship with ex #3?

12. What do you wish you had done differently during your relationship with ex #3?

13. Do you still have any contact with ex #3?

14. How do you feel about ex #3 now, and how has that changed over time?

That's it for the section on "Exorcising" Your Exes. We know how doing this work can drudge up some feelings and bad memories. If you want to talk through your experiences with your exes with other men who can relate, join us for a MAGO Gents Men's Group. You get two of them for free, but you must use them within 30 days. If you have not yet gotten on the schedule.

Scan the QR code to do so now.

SCAN ME

Change Your Luck With Women Forever

Gentlemen

Gentlemen

Part 3

Your Ideal Woman & Ideal Relationship

YOUR IDEAL WOMAN, YOUR IDEAL RELATIONSHIP

Welcome back, now we can start getting into the fun part of this work.

Name three celebrities you've always found sexy or fantasized about, and for each, describe what about them you find most attractive.

Celebrity 1.

Most attractive feature-

Celebrity 2.

Most attractive feature

Celebrity 3.

Most attractive feature

Change Your Luck With Women Forever

YOUR IDEAL WOMAN, YOUR IDEAL RELATIONSHIP

Rank the following list of **physical attributes** based on what you find most attractive. Select your top ten and number each one from 1 to 10, with 1 being the most important physical feature, 10 for the least important. There is also a space for "Other", please fill it with a physical attribute that you find attractive that is not listed.

◯	Breasts	◯	Hair
◯	Butt	◯	Feet
◯	Legs	◯	Hands
◯	Face	◯	Ears
◯	Eyes	◯	Neck
◯	Lips	◯	Shoulders
◯	Cheekbones	◯	Waistline
◯	Posture	◯	Hips
◯	Skin	◯	Muscle tone
◯	Other _____		

YOUR IDEAL WOMAN, YOUR IDEAL RELATIONSHIP

Choose from the following list to rank the three **body types** you prefer, number them in order of preference from 1 to 3. Do not number a selection unless it is in your top three...

- ◯ Thin
- ◯ Athletic (fit & toned)
- ◯ Average
- ◯ A few extra pounds
- ◯ Thick
- ◯ Heavy

What is the ideal height range? ◯ to ◯

Rank the following list of **ethnic groups**, listing up to 3 that you prefer in order of your preference, with 1 being your top preference. Do not number a selection unless it is in your top three...

- ◯ White
- ◯ Black
- ◯ Asian
- ◯ Amerindian/Alaska native
- ◯ Native Hawaiian/Pacific Islander
- ◯ Mixed Ethnicity
- ◯ Latino / Hispanic
- ◯ Middle Eastern / Arabic

YOUR IDEAL WOMAN, YOUR IDEAL RELATIONSHIP

Rank the **personality characteristics** from the list below based on what you find most attractive. Enter 1 for the most important personality trait, 10 for the least important.

- ( ) Confidence
- ( ) Sense of humor
- ( ) Intelligence
- ( ) Kindness
- ( ) Empathy
- ( ) Emotional stability
- ( ) Positive attitude
- ( ) Independence

- ( ) Humility
- ( ) Self-awareness
- ( ) Generosity/giving
- ( ) Affectonate
- ( ) Caring
- ( ) Patience
- ( ) Open-mindedness
- ( ) Supportiveness

What personality characteristic is not on this list that you find essential?

What qualities do you want in a partner that were missing in your previous relationships?

YOUR IDEAL WOMAN, YOUR IDEAL RELATIONSHIP

What are some hobbies, personal interests and pursuits that you would like to have in common with your future partner?

What are your long-term goals for a relationship and how do you see them being achieved?

What kind of lifestyle do you envision for yourself in the future and how does your future partner fit into that lifestyle?

YOUR IDEAL WOMAN, YOUR IDEAL RELATIONSHIP

What role does pornography play in your life?

Do you watch it and if so, how often?

Has it caused any problems for you in your relationships?

YOUR IDEAL WOMAN, YOUR IDEAL RELATIONSHIP

What are your love languages (top 2) and how do you express and receive love?
If you have never taken a love languages quiz, take it here
https://5lovelanguages.com/quizzes/love-language

What kind of support do you expect from your partner?

How do you see your partner fitting in with your family and friends?

YOUR IDEAL WOMAN, YOUR IDEAL RELATIONSHIP

What is your attachment style and how do you see it affecting your relationships? If you are not familiar with your attachment style, take the attachment style quiz here https://www.attachmentproject.com/attachment-style-quiz/

How do you communicate your needs and wants to your partner?

How would you handle conflict in a future relationship?

YOUR IDEAL WOMAN, YOUR IDEAL RELATIONSHIP

What are the five most important qualities you are looking for in a partner?

1.

2.

3.

4.

5.

What are your top 3 deal-breakers that you want to avoid in your future partner?

1.

2.

3.

What are the "red flags" that you will watch out for to be able to spot those three dealbreakers?

Gentlemen™

Gentlemen

Change Your Luck With Women Forever

Part 4

Evaluating Your Values

THE VALUE OF EVALUATING YOUR VALUES, A POWERFUL PONDERING OF YOUR PRINCIPLES

This workbook will focus on discovering what you value. Personal values are the core beliefs, principles, and ideals that guide our thoughts, choices, and actions. They include deeply held convictions that shape our behavior and provide a framework for decision-making.

Personal values reflect what's most important and meaningful to each of us. This influences our priorities, relationships, and overall sense of purpose and fulfillment in life. These values can be ethical, moral, cultural, or philosophical in nature and serve as a compass for navigating life's challenges, determining our goals, directing our time and money, and shaping our character and identity.

Personal values are subjective and they are unique to each person. Your values are shaped by your upbringing, experiences, culture, and personal reflection. Having a "values match" with the women you want to be in a relationship with is one of the most crucial pillars of having a solid relationship. It starts with understanding your values and the values you value.

THE VALUE OF EVALUATING YOUR VALUES, A POWERFUL PONDERING OF YOUR PRINCIPLES

1. What gives you a sense of purpose and meaning in life?

2. Describe one of the experiences (or moments) of your adult life that has brought you the most joy and fulfillment in detail. What about that experience makes it the most joyful?

THE VALUE OF EVALUATING YOUR VALUES, A POWERFUL PONDERING OF YOUR PRINCIPLES

3. Write about a big decision that you made by your own choice (but were not forced to make). What beliefs do you hold that guided your decision and actions? And why did you make the decision you made?

Decision:

Beliefs:

Why:

4. Think about a time where you were forced to make a big change under duress or had to go along with someone else's decision (even though you did not agree with it).

a) What beliefs do you hold that guided your decision and actions?

b) What did you compromise by going along with that?

THE VALUE OF EVALUATING YOUR VALUES, A POWERFUL PONDERING OF YOUR PRINCIPLES

5. Think of three people who you most love and admire. What are the traits you admire most in each of them? Enter their first name, and then list the traits that person embodies below.

Name:

Traits:

Name:

Traits:

Name:

Traits:

THE VALUE OF EVALUATING YOUR VALUES, A POWERFUL PONDERING OF YOUR PRINCIPLES

6. What causes, charities or issues do you feel most passionate about and want to support?

7. What kind of legacy do you want to leave behind?

8. What are some of your non-negotiable standards... Things that you refuse to compromise on?

Change Your Luck With Women Forever

THE VALUE OF EVALUATING YOUR VALUES, A POWERFUL PONDERING OF YOUR PRINCIPLES

9. Tell us about the last time you had an argument with someone. What principal were you fighting over?

10. Name five things that have made you feel proud of yourself.

1.

2.

3.

4.

5.

THE VALUE OF EVALUATING YOUR VALUES, A POWERFUL PONDERING OF YOUR PRINCIPLES

11. If you were to die today, and eulogize yourself... What would you say in your own eulogy?

12. If you could be remembered for only one thing, what do you want to be remembered for?

13. Now keeping your eulogy in mind... hypothetically, you are diagnosed with a terminal illness... in this scenario, you get exactly 3 months to live and you will be healthy for those three months... but in 90 days, you will keel over and pass away. Describe in detail how you are going to spend that time.

THE VALUE OF EVALUATING YOUR VALUES, A POWERFUL PONDERING OF YOUR PRINCIPLES

14. An anonymous benefactor just deposited $5 Million into your checking account.With the instructions that it must all be spent within 24 hours. What will you do with the money?

15. What will you never compromise on regardless of anything or anyone? Then ask "Why" 7 times.

I will never compromise on

Why

Why

Why

Why

Why

Why

Why

THE VALUE OF EVALUATING YOUR VALUES, A POWERFUL PONDERING OF YOUR PRINCIPLES

16. Describe one area of conflict or dissatisfaction in your life.

17. Describe the last time you were disappointed by someone in detail. Who were you disappointed by and what happened?

18. What are your "pet peeves"?

Circle 10 to 20 words from the following list that are things you value.

Accountability
Accuracy
Achievement
Action
Adaptability
Adventure
Affection
Alone Time
Altruism
Ambition
Animal Rights
Appreciation
Artistry
Authenticity
Autonomy
Awareness
Balance
Beauty
Boldness
Bravery
Calm / Calmness
Caring
Charisma
Charity
Change
Changing the World
Cleverness
Clarity
Cleanliness
Coaching
Cooperation
Community
Confidence
Conformity
Connection/Relationships
Consciousness
Constructive Criticism
Contribution
Courage
Credibility
Creativity
Culture
Curiosity
Dedication
Deep Connections
Dependability
Discipline
Diversity
Dynamism / Dynamic Responses

Education
Emotional intelligence
Empathy
Encouragement
Energy
Enthusiasm
Environmental Protection
Experimentation
Experiences
Equality
Fame
Family
Faith
Faithfulness
Fast Pace
Financial Security
Fitness
Finesse
Flexibility
Forgiveness
Fortitude
Freedom
Friendliness
Friendship
Fulfillment
Generosity
Gentleness
Gift-Giving
Goodness
Gracefulness
Gratitude
Growth Mindset
Hard Work Ethic
Harmony
Health/Fitness
Happiness
Honesty
Honor
Hope
Humility
Humor
Ideas
Implementation
Independence
Influence
Ingenuity
Innovation
Insightfulness
Integrity
Intellectual stimulation

Intimacy
Intuition
Joy
Justice
Kindness
Knowledge
Legacy
Liveliness
Listening
Love
Management
Mentorship
Meaningful work
Modesty
Mutual Support
Natural Living
Nature
Non-Conformity
Non-Violence
Open-Mindedness
Openness
Optimism
Originality
Organization
Patience
Passion
Peace of Mind
Peacefulness
Persistence
Personal Achievement
Personal Development
Personal Expression
Planning
Playfulness
Positive Attitude
Positive Impact
Power
Problem-Solving
Professionalism
Profit
Promise-keeping
Protection
Quality
Quality Time
Reciprocity
Recognition
Reliability
Religion
Respect
Resourcefulness

Restraint
Righteousness Romance
Safety
Self-Control
Self-Development
Self-Discipline
Selflessness
Self-Expression
Self-Improvement
Self-Development
Self-Love
Self-Motivation
Self-Preservation
Service to Others
Sex
Showing Appreciation
Socializing
Social Justice
Spirituality
Spontaneity
Stability
Stewardship
Strength
Sustainability
Sweetness
Teamwork
Thrift
Thoughtfulness Tidiness
Tolerance
Tradition
Transparency
Travel
Trust
Trusting Your Gut
Trustworthiness
Understanding
Uniqueness
Vivaciousness
Wealth
Wellness
Wit
Work
Work-Life Balance
Working Smarter, Not Harder

Change Your Luck With Women Forever

Underline 10 things from the following list that you have spent the most money on in the past year. (Do not refer to the previous list you just circled.)

Accountability
Accuracy
Achievement
Action
Adaptability
Adventure
Affection
Alone Time
Altruism
Ambition
Animal Rights
Appreciation
Artistry
Authenticity
Autonomy
Awareness
Balance
Beauty
Boldness
Bravery
Calm / Calmness
Caring
Charisma
Charity
Change
Changing the World
Cleverness
Clarity
Cleanliness
Coaching
Cooperation
Community
Confidence
Conformity
Connection/Relationships
Consciousness
Constructive Criticism
Contribution
Courage
Credibility
Creativity
Culture
Curiosity
Dedication
Deep Connections
Dependability
Discipline
Diversity
Dynamism / Dynamic Responses

Education
Emotional intelligence
Empathy
Encouragement
Energy
Enthusiasm
Environmental Protection
Experimentation
Experiences
Equality
Fame
Family
Faith
Faithfulness
Fast Pace
Financial Security
Fitness
Finesse
Flexibility
Forgiveness
Fortitude
Freedom
Friendliness
Friendship
Fulfillment
Generosity
Gentleness
Gift-Giving
Goodness
Gracefulness
Gratitude
Growth Mindset
Hard Work Ethic
Harmony
Health/Fitness
Happiness
Honesty
Honor
Hope
Humility
Humor
Ideas
Implementation
Independence
Influence
Ingenuity
Innovation
Insightfulness
Integrity
Intellectual stimulation

Intimacy
Intuition
Joy
Justice
Kindness
Knowledge
Legacy
Liveliness
Listening
Love
Management
Mentorship
Meaningful work
Modesty
Mutual Support
Natural Living
Nature
Non-Conformity
Non-Violence
Open-Mindedness
Openness
Optimism
Originality
Organization
Patience
Passion
Peace of Mind
Peacefulness
Persistence
Personal Achievement
Personal Development
Personal Expression
Planning
Playfulness
Positive Attitude
Positive Impact
Power
Problem-Solving
Professionalism
Profit
Promise-keeping
Protection
Quality
Quality Time
Reciprocity
Recognition
Reliability
Religion
Respect
Resourcefulness

Restraint
Righteousness Romance
Safety
Self-Control
Self-Development
Self-Discipline
Selflessness
Self-Expression
Self-Improvement
Self-Development
Self-Love
Self-Motivation
Self-Preservation
Service to Others
Sex
Showing Appreciation
Socializing
Social Justice
Spirituality
Spontaneity
Stability
Stewardship
Strength
Sustainability
Sweetness
Teamwork
Thrift
Thoughtfulness Tidiness
Tolerance
Tradition
Transparency
Travel
Trust
Trusting Your Gut
Trustworthiness
Understanding
Uniqueness
Vivaciousness
Wealth
Wellness
Wit
Work
Work-Life Balance
Working Smarter, Not Harder

NOTES & REFLECTIONS

NOTES & REFLECTIONS

Change Your Luck With Women Forever

Part 5

What Do You You Want?

SO WHAT'CHA, WHAT'CHA, WHAT'CHA WANT? (WHAT'CHA WANT?)

In this section, we're going to get a very clear picture of what you want in life (and in your future relationship). Only when you are crystal clear on what you want will you be able to attract your ideal woman to your life.

It's going to be helpful for you to refer to the previous sections of the workbook as you do your work this week. Remember to answer the questions in the workbook honestly and candidly. It should take you approximately 3 hours to complete this section.

SO WHAT'CHA, WHAT'CHA, WHAT'CHA WANT? (WHAT'CHA WANT?)

What do you want in a woman? Be specific.

What do you want FROM a woman?

What do you envision your life will look like when you have attracted your ideal woman?

SO WHAT'CHA, WHAT'CHA, WHAT'CHA WANT? (WHAT'CHA WANT?)

What will your life look like in 5 years? Describe your future vision in great detail.

What HAS TO HAPPEN within the next year for you to be on the path toward those goals?

SO WHAT'CHA, WHAT'CHA, WHAT'CHA WANT?
(WHAT'CHA WANT?)

What are the top five things on your personal bucket list?

1
2
3
4
5

What are the top 5 things you want to DO when you are in your ideal relationship?

1
2
3
4
5

SO WHAT'CHA, WHAT'CHA, WHAT'CHA WANT? (WHAT'CHA WANT?)

What are ten things you want to HAVE when you are in this relationship?

1.

2.

3.

4.

5.

6.

7.

8.

9.

10.

SO WHAT'CHA, WHAT'CHA, WHAT'CHA WANT? (WHAT'CHA WANT?)

What are five ways you want to FEEL when you are in this relationship?

1

2

3

4

5

What are 5 ways you do NOT want to feel when you are in relationship?

1

2

3

4

5

SO WHAT'CHA, WHAT'CHA, WHAT'CHA WANT? (WHAT'CHA WANT?)

Describe in detail ... Who will you BE when you are in this relationship?

How is this different from who you are right now?

What signs will you look for that will confirm for you that you are in your ideal relationship?

SO WHAT'CHA, WHAT'CHA, WHAT'CHA WANT? (WHAT'CHA WANT?)

Among your friends and family members, is there a couple who has the type of relationship you want to have? If so, describe their relationship in detail.

What are your feelings on exclusivity and monogamy?

What is your definition of cheating?

SO WHAT'CHA, WHAT'CHA, WHAT'CHA WANT? (WHAT'CHA WANT?)

What does "marriage" mean to you?

(Answer this question only If you have previously been married). Would you ever get married (again)? Why or why not?

What are your thoughts about having kids / building a family?

NOTES & REFLECTIONS

Change Your Luck With Women Forever

NOTES & REFLECTIONS

Change Your Luck With Women Forever

Part 6

Conquering Your MalBes

AS AN EXTRA BONUS...

What's a MalBe?

"MalBe" is shorthand for a Maladaptive Belief.

MalBes are bullshit.

They come from the stories we told ourselves as we tried to makes sense of painful and sometimes traumatic experiences that happened in our past.

Some of them come from situations so far removed from reality it's ridiculous. As a little kid, you might have had separation anxiety when Mommy left you at pre-school and your 4-year-old brain, trying to make sense of it, interpreted that to mean something was wrong with you...

Or perhaps your parents split up after a huge fight, and your Dad yelled at you and broke your favorite toy... and your 6-year-old brain internalized that trauma with a MalBe that made you feel unsafe.

MalBes have a significant negative impact on our self-esteem and on your overall well-being. Once a MalBe gets into our heads, it can be very tough to shake them. And frankly, our entire culture is permeated by MalBes. Advertising triggers them to make you buy.

MalBes are often unconscious, but they show up as negative thoughts and as unhealthy patterns in our relationships. It's crucial that we challenge and reframe our MalBes.

Along with the self-reflection you're about to do, this work requires countermeasures and a lot of compassion for yourself.
You might feel ashamed, sad, and upset as you do this work.

But remember, MalBes started forming when you were a little child. So, it's not your fault that you have experienced them.

For each of the following MalBes, take time to reflect and answer the questions that follow. And be sure to end this exercise with the countermeasures.

MalBe #1 - "I'm not good enough":

This belief revolves around feelings of inadequacy and a persistent sense of self-doubt. It can lead men to underestimate their abilities and accomplishments, causing them to feel unworthy of success or happiness.

Have you ever held this MalBe? Y/N

What about you is "not good enough"? Explain it in detail.

Explain how this shows up in your relationships.

What triggers this MalBe for you?

MalBe #2 - "I'm inadequate":

Similar to the previous MalBe, this one reflects a feeling of overall incompetence. It involves a deep-seated feeling of not measuring up to the standards or expectations set by oneself or others.

Have you ever held this MalBe? Y/N

What about you is "inadequate"? Explain in detail.

Explain how this shows up in your life or relationships. Give detail

What triggers it?

MalBe #3 - "People will leave me":

This belief stems from a fear of abandonment and can be rooted in past experiences of rejection or loss. The poor Gents who hold this MalBe may constantly worry that others will eventually abandon or reject them, leading to difficulties in forming and maintaining healthy relationships. Often men who harbor this MalBe are the ones who leave first, like launching a pre-emptive strike. "I'll be the one doing the leaving"

Have you ever held this MalBe? Y/N
What is the root of this? Who is the significant person from your past who left? What happened?

Explain how this MalBe has showed up in your relationships since then. Have you seen a pattern of being left or leaving?

When was the last time this MalBe was triggered for you? Explain in detail.

MalBe #4 - "I'm unsafe":

This belief involves a perception of constant threat or danger in one's environment. It can arise from past traumatic experiences or a general sense of vulnerability, leading individuals to feel anxious and hypervigilant even in relatively safe situations.

Have you ever held this MalBe? Y/N
Explain how this shows up in your life.

What triggers it now?

Can you explain what you consider the ROOT cause of this MalBe for you? When you were little, what happened that made you feel unsafe?

MalBe #5 - "I can't trust others":

This belief stems from a lack of trust in other people's intentions or reliability. It often develops as a result of past betrayals or experiences of being let down. Men who are burdened by this MalBe may struggle to form and maintain trusting relationships, which leaves a Gent with feelings of isolation.

Have you ever held this MalBe? Y/N
Explain how this shows up in your life.

Who has broken your trust? Explain in detail all the circumstances.

Have you also been a breaker of trust? Explain.

Can people trust you? Explain.

Do you trust anyone now? Who and why?

On a scale of 1 to 10, with 10 being totally trusting... how much trust can you give to your most trusted person in your life?

MalBe #6 - "I must be perfect":

This belief revolves around an unrealistic expectation of flawlessness in oneself. It can lead to intense self-criticism, fear of failure, and a constant drive for perfection, crippling self-consciousness, all of which are exhausting. This belief may contribute to anxiety, low self-esteem, and difficulty in enjoying achievements.

Have you ever held this MalBe? Y/N
Explain how this shows up in your life.

For whom did you always have to be perfect?

What were / are the consequences of imperfection?

How does it make you feel?

MalBe #7 - "I'm unworthy of love":

This belief revolves around a deep-seated conviction that a Gent is fundamentally unlovable or undeserving of love and affection. Men with this MalBe tend to push away or sabotage relationships, as they believe they don't deserve love or that it will inevitably be withdrawn.

Have you ever held this MalBe? Y/N
Explain how this shows up in your life.

What about you makes you feel that you are "unworthy" of love?

Who rejected you and broke your heart? Explain.

Who did you push away because of this MalBe? Explain.

MalBe #8 - "I'm a failure":

This belief involves a pervasive sense of being a failure in various aspects of life, such as work, relationships, or personal achievements. It often comes with harsh self-criticism, feelings of shame, and a constant focus on the perceived shortcomings. This MalBe hinders personal growth and self-confidence.

Have you ever held this MalBe? Y/N
List your top 3 biggest "failures".

For each, what did you do (or not do) that made it fail?

What has this focus on failure stopped you from trying in your life?

MalBe #9 - "I'm always to blame":

This belief centers around taking excessive responsibility for negative events or conflicts, regardless of actual culpability. Individuals holding this belief tend to internalize blame and feel excessively guilty, even in situations where they are not primarily at fault, leading to a heightened sense of self-blame and self-criticism.

Have you ever held this MalBe? Y/N
What is one major thing you are to blame for? Explain the circumstances in detail.

Describe how it shows up for you in relationships.

MalBe #10 - "I'm powerless":

This belief reflects a perception of helplessness and lack of control over one's own life and circumstances. Gentlemen with this belief may feel overwhelmed by challenges and believe they are unable to influence or change their situations, leading to a sense of resignation and diminished motivation.

Have you ever held this MalBe? Y/N
If so, describe where in your life it shows up for you, give specific examples.

List the significant things in your life that you have "no power" over.

If you had power over one of them, what would you do?

MalBe #11 - "I must please others":

This is a very common MalBe. This belief revolves around an excessive need for approval and validation from others. Individuals holding this belief often prioritize the happiness and opinions of others over their own needs and desires, leading to a diminished sense of self and difficulty asserting personal boundaries. If you lived by the credo "Happy wife. Happy life." You've experienced this MalBe.

Have you ever held this MalBe? Y/N
If you answered yes, to what lengths do you go to please others?

Have you ever tried to please someone, but no matter what you did you could not? Explain in detail.

What did it cost you?

MalBe #12 - "I'm inherently flawed":

This belief involves a deeply ingrained belief that there is something fundamentally wrong or defective about oneself. It can lead to a persistent sense of shame and self-loathing. When a Gentleman views himself as irreparably flawed, it greatly impacts their self-esteem and overall well-being.

What "inherent flaws" do you possess? Describe them in detail.

If you could change these "flaws", would you? Y / N
Describe in detail what you would change.

Now Take Countermeasures...

When we read phrases like "I'm Powerless" or "I'm unworthy of love", we are literally programming ourselves with negative, soul-crushing, self-esteem destroying bullshit

We don't want to reinforce our MalBes

Using the simple affirmations and exercises (see examples) below can help you cancel negative, self-defeating patterns, and may even help you eradicate your MalBes over time. You can use these to counter your MalBes every time they come up. Your coach and group facilitator can help.

Below is an incomplete list of countermeasures we can use to reprogram ourselves. Schedule some time with your MAGO Gents Coach for countermeasures specific to the MalBes you're dealing with.

EXAMPLE COUNTERMEASURES -

MalBe #1 Not Good Enough

If you suffer from the not-good enough MalBe, say the following affirmations out loud 20 times while looking in the mirror...

"I am enough just as I am."

Say this affirmation multiple times a day. Say it EVERY TIME that "I'm not good enough" comes up for you. Every time you look in a mirror. Say it with a smile. It may feel weird at first. But, you will soon feel okay saying it. And you'll learn to use it as a counterpunch to knock this MalBe out.

Tip: Take out a notebook and cover an entire page with the same affirmation, "I am enough just as I am." Write it over and over again.

Bonus affirmations...

- I am inherently worthy and I deserve love.
- I am inherently worthy and I deserve happiness.
- I am inherently worthy and I deserve success.
- I embrace my unique qualities, strengths, and imperfections.
- I trust in myself and my abilities.

MalBe #3 Being left / abandoned.

Prescribed countermeasures:

Talk about the root cause with your coach and in your next group.

Do the Forgiveness Exercise (ask your MAGO Group Facilitator)

Self-compassion and self-care are so important to Gents who are afflicted with this MalBe. Make plans to take yourself out to do whatever it is your heart desires. On your own. Whatever it is. Take yourself on a date.

There is almost always another MalBe that accompanies this one, so whichever it is, also perform that countermeasure.

MalBe #11 People-Pleasing

The first countermeasure we recommend here is to read Dr Robert Glover's book, No More Mr Nice Guy. One of our favorites.

Say "No" to something. Anything. It can be small. It should be something you would normally go along with, but really don't want to.

Schedule time with your MAGO Gents Coach to get the countermeasures for any of the remaining MalBes not covered in the examples above.

Gentlemen

Gentlemen

The 10 First
Dates Challenge

We're about to look at how your dating results match up with you really want in a woman.

Your work now is to compare your real-life dating experiences to the work you've done in this workbook so far.

As you fill these sections in, you'll want refer to the previous sections in the workbook.

This part of the program is where you "spread your wings" and put into practice all that you have discovered by doing DEEP WORK. Remember, our Lifeline service is available to you anytime you need a Sage Wingman to give you on-the-spot dating advice, just reach out to us at support@magogents.com for details.

DATE #1

Answer the following questions about each woman.

DATE #1   (Her Name)

Describe her and explain why you decided to ask her on the date.

What did you do on your date?

What was your first impression of her?

DATE #1

How did you FEEL about her?

Where and how did you connect with her?

Did you decide to ask her out on another date? Why or why not?

Change Your Luck With Women Forever

DATE #1

Now, consider her in comparison to your earlier work on Your Ideal Woman, and assign a number from 1 to 10 with 10 being the highest on how closely she matched your ideal overall.

Number: [ ]

How many of the five most important qualities (Page 36 of this Workbook) does she possess?

Number: [ ]

Did you see ANY of your "red flag dealbreakers"? Y/N If so, in what way did they show up?

[ ]

Refer back to the section on Evaluating Your Values...

In comparison to the work on your values, assign a number from 1 to 10 with 10 being the highest on how closely she matches your values.

Number: [ ]

DATE #1

If you continue to date her, would you be compromising on any of your values and if so, in what way(s)?

General notes on this date:

DATE #2

Answer the following questions about each woman.

DATE #2   (Her Name)

Describe her and explain why you decided to ask her on the date.

What did you do on your date?

What was your first impression of her?

DATE #2

How did you FEEL about her?

Where and how did you connect with her?

Did you decide to ask her out on another date? Why or why not?

DATE #2

Now, consider her in comparison to your earlier work on Your Ideal Woman, and assign a number from 1 to 10 with 10 being the highest on how closely she matched your ideal overall.

Number: [ ]

How many of the five most important qualities (Page 36 of this Workbook) does she possess?

Number: [ ]

Did you see ANY of your "red flag dealbreakers"? Y/N If so, in what way did they show up?

[ ]

Refer back to the section on Evaluating Your Values...

In comparison to the work on your values, assign a number from 1 to 10 with 10 being the highest on how closely she matches your values.

Number: [ ]

DATE #2

If you continue to date her, would you be compromising on any of your values and if so, in what way(s)?

General notes on this date:

Change Your Luck With Women Forever

DATE #3

Answer the following questions about each woman.

DATE #3   (Her Name)

Describe her and explain why you decided to ask her on the date.

What did you do on your date?

What was your first impression of her?

DATE #3

How did you FEEL about her?

Where and how did you connect with her?

Did you decide to ask her out on another date? Why or why not?

Change Your Luck With Women Forever

DATE #3

Now, consider her in comparison to your earlier work on Your Ideal Woman, and assign a number from 1 to 10 with 10 being the highest on how closely she matched your ideal overall.

Number: [ ]

How many of the five most important qualities (Page 36 of this Workbook) does she possess?

Number: [ ]

Did you see ANY of your "red flag dealbreakers"? Y/N If so, in what way did they show up?

[ ]

Refer back to the section on Evaluating Your Values...

In comparison to the work on your values, assign a number from 1 to 10 with 10 being the highest on how closely she matches your values.

Number: [ ]

Change Your Luck With Women Forever

DATE #3

If you continue to date her, would you be compromising on any of your values and if so, in what way(s)?

General notes on this date:

Change Your Luck With Women Forever

DATE #4

Answer the following questions about each woman.

DATE #4   (Her Name)

Describe her and explain why you decided to ask her on the date.

What did you do on your date?

What was your first impression of her?

DATE #4

How did you FEEL about her?

Where and how did you connect with her?

Did you decide to ask her out on another date? Why or why not?

DATE #4

Now, consider her in comparison to your earlier work on Your Ideal Woman, and assign a number from 1 to 10 with 10 being the highest on how closely she matched your ideal overall.

Number: ☐

How many of the five most important qualities (Page 36 of this Workbook) does she possess?

Number: ☐

Did you see ANY of your "red flag dealbreakers"? Y/N If so, in what way did they show up?

☐

Refer back to the section on Evaluating Your Values...

In comparison to the work on your values, assign a number from 1 to 10 with 10 being the highest on how closely she matches your values.

Number: ☐

DATE #4

If you continue to date her, would you be compromising on any of your values and if so, in what way(s)?

General notes on this date:

Change Your Luck With Women Forever

DATE #5

Answer the following questions about each woman.

DATE #5   (Her Name)

Describe her and explain why you decided to ask her on the date.

What did you do on your date?

What was your first impression of her?

DATE #5

How did you FEEL about her?

Where and how did you connect with her?

Did you decide to ask her out on another date? Why or why not?

Change Your Luck With Women Forever

DATE #5

Now, consider her in comparison to your earlier work on Your Ideal Woman, and assign a number from 1 to 10 with 10 being the highest on how closely she matched your ideal overall.

Number: [ ]

How many of the five most important qualities (Page 36 of this Workbook) does she possess?

Number: [ ]

Did you see ANY of your "red flag dealbreakers"? Y/N If so, in what way did they show up?

[ ]

Refer back to the section on Evaluating Your Values...

In comparison to the work on your values, assign a number from 1 to 10 with 10 being the highest on how closely she matches your values.

Number: [ ]

DATE #5

If you continue to date her, would you be compromising on any of your values and if so, in what way(s)?

General notes on this date:

DATE #6

Answer the following questions about each woman.

DATE #6　　(Her Name)

Describe her and explain why you decided to ask her on the date.

What did you do on your date?

What was your first impression of her?

DATE #6

How did you FEEL about her?

Where and how did you connect with her?

Did you decide to ask her out on another date? Why or why not?

Change Your Luck With Women Forever

DATE #6

Now, consider her in comparison to your earlier work on Your Ideal Woman, and assign a number from 1 to 10 with 10 being the highest on how closely she matched your ideal overall.

Number: [ ]

How many of the five most important qualities (Page 36 of this Workbook) does she possess?

Number: [ ]

Did you see ANY of your "red flag dealbreakers"? Y/N If so, in what way did they show up?

[ ]

Refer back to the section on Evaluating Your Values...

In comparison to the work on your values, assign a number from 1 to 10 with 10 being the highest on how closely she matches your values.

Number: [ ]

DATE #6

If you continue to date her, would you be compromising on any of your values and if so, in what way(s)?

General notes on this date:

Change Your Luck With Women Forever

DATE #7

Answer the following questions about each woman.

DATE #7   (Her Name)

Describe her and explain why you decided to ask her on the date.

What did you do on your date?

What was your first impression of her?

DATE #7

How did you FEEL about her?

Where and how did you connect with her?

Did you decide to ask her out on another date? Why or why not?

DATE #7

Now, consider her in comparison to your earlier work on Your Ideal Woman, and assign a number from 1 to 10 with 10 being the highest on how closely she matched your ideal overall.

Number: [　]

How many of the five most important qualities (Page 36 of this Workbook) does she possess?

Number: [　]

Did you see ANY of your "red flag dealbreakers"? Y/N If so, in what way did they show up?

[　]

Refer back to the section on Evaluating Your Values...

In comparison to the work on your values, assign a number from 1 to 10 with 10 being the highest on how closely she matches your values.

Number: [　]

DATE #7

If you continue to date her, would you be compromising on any of your values and if so, in what way(s)?

General notes on this date:

DATE #8

Answer the following questions about each woman.

DATE #8   (Her Name)

Describe her and explain why you decided to ask her on the date.

What did you do on your date?

What was your first impression of her?

DATE #8

How did you FEEL about her?

Where and how did you connect with her?

Did you decide to ask her out on another date? Why or why not?

Change Your Luck With Women Forever

DATE #8

Now, consider her in comparison to your earlier work on Your Ideal Woman, and assign a number from 1 to 10 with 10 being the highest on how closely she matched your ideal overall.

Number: [ ]

How many of the five most important qualities (Page 36 of this Workbook) does she possess?

Number: [ ]

Did you see ANY of your "red flag dealbreakers"? Y/N If so, in what way did they show up?

[ ]

Refer back to the section on Evaluating Your Values...

In comparison to the work on your values, assign a number from 1 to 10 with 10 being the highest on how closely she matches your values.

Number: [ ]

DATE #8

If you continue to date her, would you be compromising on any of your values and if so, in what way(s)?

General notes on this date:

Change Your Luck With Women Forever

DATE #9

Answer the following questions about each woman.

DATE #9   (Her Name)

Describe her and explain why you decided to ask her on the date.

What did you do on your date?

What was your first impression of her?

DATE #9

How did you FEEL about her?

Where and how did you connect with her?

Did you decide to ask her out on another date? Why or why not?

DATE #9

Now, consider her in comparison to your earlier work on Your Ideal Woman, and assign a number from 1 to 10 with 10 being the highest on how closely she matched your ideal overall.

Number: [ ]

How many of the five most important qualities (Page 36 of this Workbook) does she possess?

Number: [ ]

Did you see ANY of your "red flag dealbreakers"? Y/N If so, in what way did they show up?

[ ]

Refer back to the section on Evaluating Your Values...

In comparison to the work on your values, assign a number from 1 to 10 with 10 being the highest on how closely she matches your values.

Number: [ ]

Change Your Luck With Women Forever

DATE #9

If you continue to date her, would you be compromising on any of your values and if so, in what way(s)?

General notes on this date:

DATE #10

Answer the following questions about each woman.

DATE #10   (Her Name)

Describe her and explain why you decided to ask her on the date.

What did you do on your date?

What was your first impression of her?

DATE #10

How did you FEEL about her?

Where and how did you connect with her?

Did you decide to ask her out on another date? Why or why not?

DATE #10

Now, consider her in comparison to your earlier work on Your Ideal Woman, and assign a number from 1 to 10 with 10 being the highest on how closely she matched your ideal overall.

Number: [ ]

How many of the five most important qualities (Page 36 of this Workbook) does she possess?

Number: [ ]

Did you see ANY of your "red flag dealbreakers"? Y/N If so, in what way did they show up?

[ ]

Refer back to the section on Evaluating Your Values...

In comparison to the work on your values, assign a number from 1 to 10 with 10 being the highest on how closely she matches your values.

Number: [ ]

DATE #10

If you continue to date her, would you be compromising on any of your values and if so, in what way(s)?

General notes on this date:

Change Your Luck With Women Forever

NOTES & REFLECTIONS

NOTES & REFLECTIONS

Change Your Luck With Women Forever

www.ingramcontent.com/pod-product-compliance
Lightning Source LLC
Chambersburg PA
CBHW080335270326
41927CB00014B/3233